CELINE DION A NEW DAY HAS COME

International Consultant: Ben Kaye

Management: Rene Angelil
FEELING PRODUCTIONS INC.
In Montreal:
2540 Boulevard Daniel-Johnson, #755
Laval, Quebec
Canada H7T 2S3

In Toronto:
1131A Leslie Street, Penthouse #5
Toronto, Ontario
Canada M3C 3L8
Management Contact: Dave Platel

Business Affairs: Paul Farberman

Celine Dion International Fan Club
P.O. Box 551
Don Mills, Ontario
Canada M3C 2T6

*Special thanks to Ben Kaye and Feeling Productions for these past seven years
of direction, patience, and confidence in Warner Bros. Publications. May our
combined efforts continue to produce many more beautiful books for years to
come. Congratulations on another great album.*

Carol Cuellar
Director
Popular Music

Book Art Layout: Nancy Rehm
Album Artwork: © 2002 Sony Music Entertainment (Canada) Inc.
Cover Photography: Patrick Demarchelier
Additional Photography: Gerard Schachmes and Laurent Cayla

I'M ALIVE

Words and Music by
KRISTIAN LUNDIN and ANDREAS CARLSSON

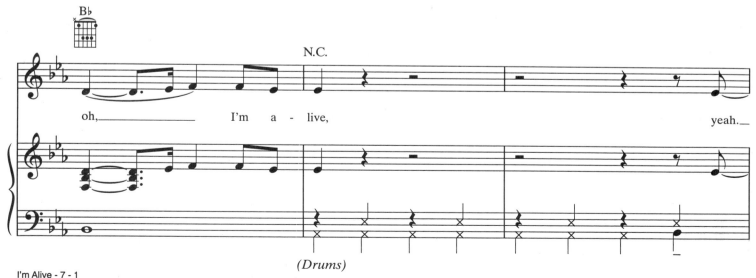

could - n't get much high - er, my spir - it___ takes flight,___

___ 'cause I'm___ a - live,___ oh.___ When you

Coda

Bridge:

knows___ that,___ that I'll be___ the one stand - ing

by through good and___ through try - ing___ times.___

RIGHT IN FRONT OF YOU

Words and Music by
STEVE MORALES, SHEP SOLOMAN,
KARA DIOGUARDI and DAVID SIEGEL

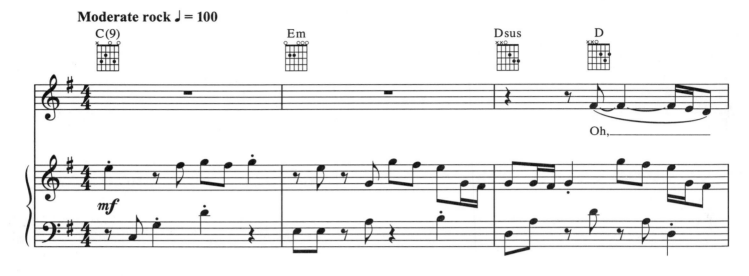

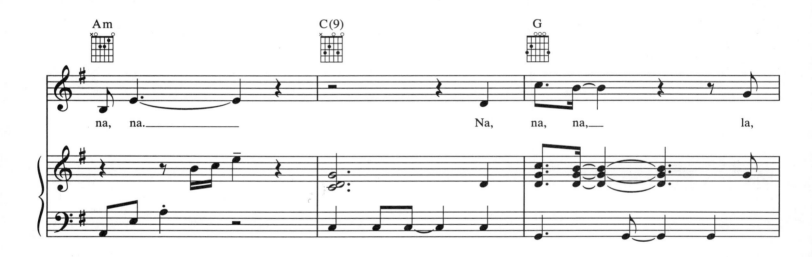

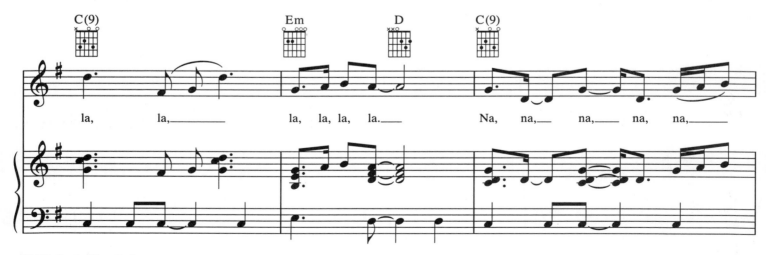

Right in Front of You - 8 - 1
0682B

18

Chorus:

HAVE YOU EVER BEEN IN LOVE

Words and Music by
PAR ASTROM,
THOMAS MARK HARMER NICHOLS,
ANDERS SVEN BAGGE,
DARYL HALL and LAILA BAGGE

Freely, with feeling

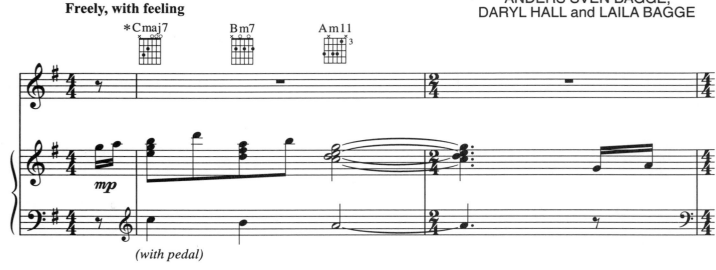

(with pedal)

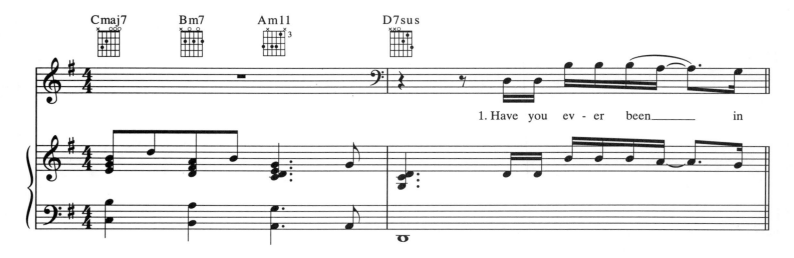

1. Have you ev-er been_____ in

Moderately slow ♩ = 69

Verse:

love?
air?

You could touch_____ the moon-
Ev - er felt like you_____ were dream-

* Original recording in G♭ major.

A NEW DAY HAS COME
(Radio Remix)

Words and Music by
STEPHAN MOCCIO and ALDO NOVA

* **Moderate dance tempo** ♩ = 120

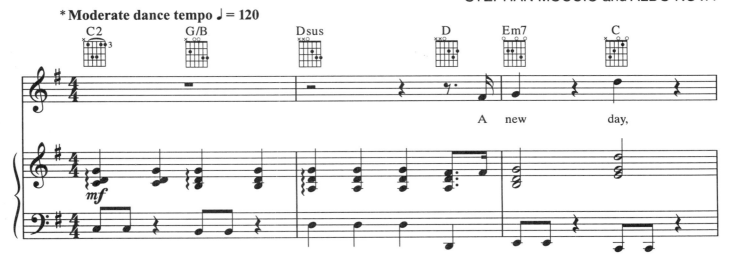

A new day,

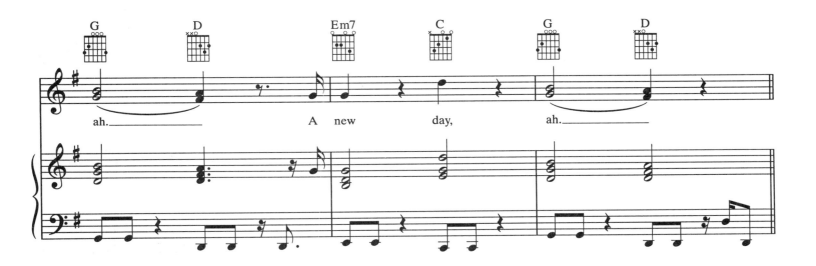

ah._____ A new day, ah._____

Verse 1:

1. I was wait - ing__ for so long, for a mir - a - cle__ to

* Original recording 1/2 step down in G♭ (E♭ minor).

A New Day Has Come (Radio Remix) - 5 - 1
0682B

A New Day Has Come (Radio Remix) - 5 - 3
0682B

34

A New Day Has Come (Radio Remix) - 5 - 4
0682B

RAIN, TAX
(It's Inevitable)

Words and Music by
TERRY BRITTEN and CHARLIE DOVE

38

Chorus:

TEN DAYS

Words and Music by
ALDO NOVA, MAXIME LE FORESTIER,
GÉRALD DE PALMAS

GOODBYE'S
(The Saddest Word)

Words and Music by
R.J. LANGE

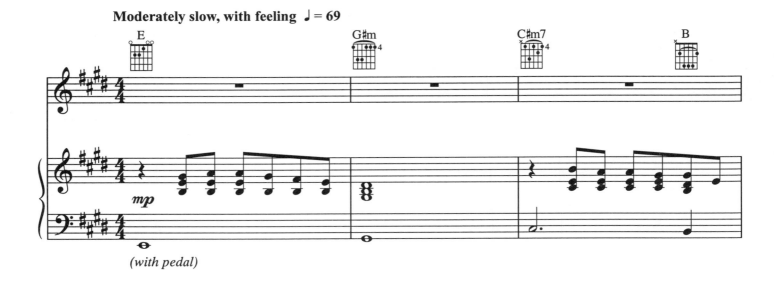

Verse:

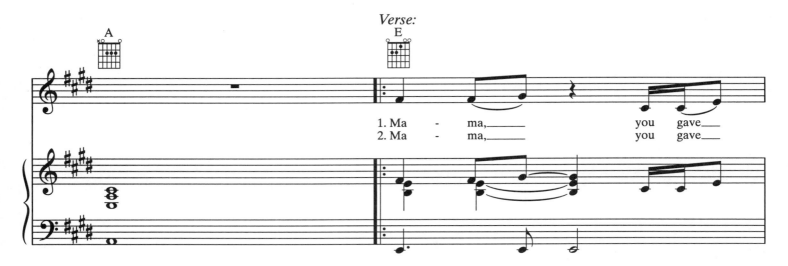

1. Ma - ma, you gave
2. Ma - ma, you gave

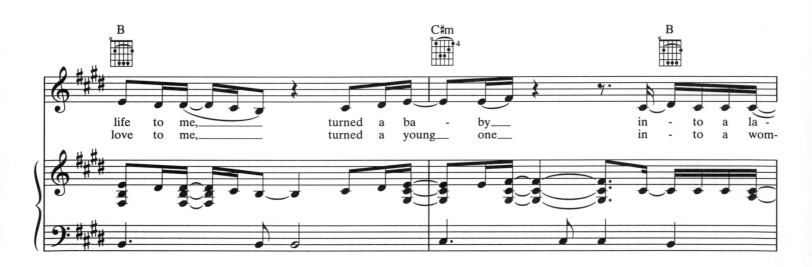

life to me, turned a ba - by in - to a la -
love to me, turned a young one in - to a wom-

Goodbye's (The Saddest Word) - 8 - 1
0682B

PRAYER

Words and Music by
COREY HART

Slow ballad ♩ = 72

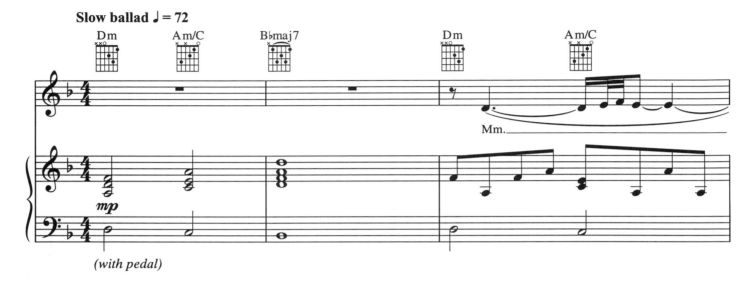

(with pedal)

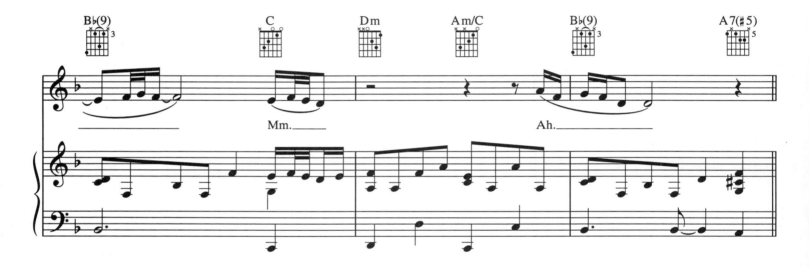

Verse:

1. Can we touch the soul__ of heav-en? Can we u-nite a sa-cred les-son?
2. *See additional lyrics*

mp - mf

58

Yet the prom-ised chance___ re - mains,___ gifts of what__ could be.___

To Next Strain

1. So, let the ___ 2. Let the

℀ Chorus:

(1. 2.) chil - dren re - mem - ber the sun.___ Let them dance, let them soar,___ for their lives_
(3.) chil - dren for they__ are the light.___ They are the truth__ of

___ have be - gun.___ Let the chil - dren en - gen - der the rain,_____ as the
spir - it in flight._ Yes, the chil - dren en - gen - der the rain,_____ as the

Prayer - 6 - 3
0682B

Verse 2:
Ev'ry voice along the shoreline,
Standing still within time,
Spinning unresolved the walking.
As each season passes,
Through wonderland, looking glasses,
The secret garden shire beckons you.
Gentle flower, don't fade away.
Sweet innocent still harbors thee
In the faith of golden dreams,
Where one love lives eternally.
(To Chorus 2:)

I SURRENDER

Words and Music by
LOUIS BIANCANIELLO and SAM WATTERS

* Original recording in key of G# minor.

I Surrender - 8 - 1
0682B

66

I Surrender - 8 - 5
0682B

AT LAST

Music by
MACK GORDON
Lyrics by
HARRY WARREN

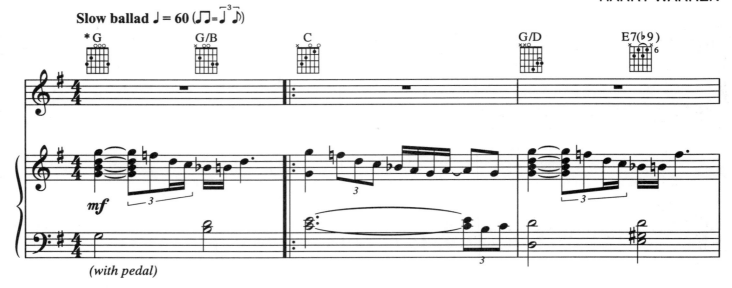

* Original recording in key of F♯ major.

72

SORRY FOR LOVE

Words and Music by
KARA DIOGUARDI, ANDERS BAGGE,
PAR ASHTON and ARNTHOR BIRGISSON

1. For-give me for the things_____ that I nev-er said_____ to you.
2. Or may-be there've been times_____ that I let you_____ down.

78

Chorus:

AÚN EXISTE AMOR

Music by RICHARD COCCIANTE
Original French Lyrics by LUC PLAMONDON
Spanish Adaptation by IGNACIO BALLESTEROS-DIAZ

(with pedal)

Cuan - do__ te_a-dor-me - ces jun-to_a__ mí,__ en - ton-ces no me que - dan du -

das,__ de que_aún e - xis - te_a - mor.__ La_in-de - ci - sión que hay__ en mí,

yo la man-da-ré_a__ la lu - na__ pa - ra vi - vir con-ti -

THE GREATEST REWARD

Words and Music by
PASCAL OBISPO, ANDREAS CARLSSON,
JÖRGEN ELOFSSON, LIONEL FIORENCE
and PATRICE GUIRAO

Verses 2 & 3:

Verse 4:

WHEN THE WRONG ONE LOVES YOU RIGHT

Words and Music by
MARTIN BRILEY, FRANCIS GALLUCCIO
and MARJORIE MAYE

1. I don't care what they think, how they feel, what they say,____
2. *See additional lyrics*

Verse 2:
Getting tired of hearing that
You're dangerous, but they won't stop.
Until I leave, they won't believe
That being with you won't break my heart.
So worried 'bout the road ahead,
They can't see that you're my best friend.
They're never gonna take me away from you.
There's nothing they can do.
(To Chorus:)

A NEW DAY HAS COME

Words and Music by
STEPHAN MOCCIO and ALDO NOVA

* Original recording 1/2 step down in G♭ (E♭ minor).

A New Day Has Come - 8 - 1
0682B

100

C(9) Em7 D

hold on and don't shed a tear.

Verses 2 & 3:

Em C/E G/D D

2. Through the dark - ness and good times,
3. Where it was dark, now there's light.

Em C/E G/D D

I knew I'd make it through.
Where there was pain, now there's joy.

Em C/E G/D D

And the world thought I had it all, but
Where there was weak - ness, I had found my strength

A New Day Has Come - 8 - 3
0682B

102

NATURE BOY

Slowly & freely (♩ = 72)

Words and Music by
EDEN AHBEZ

There was a boy,

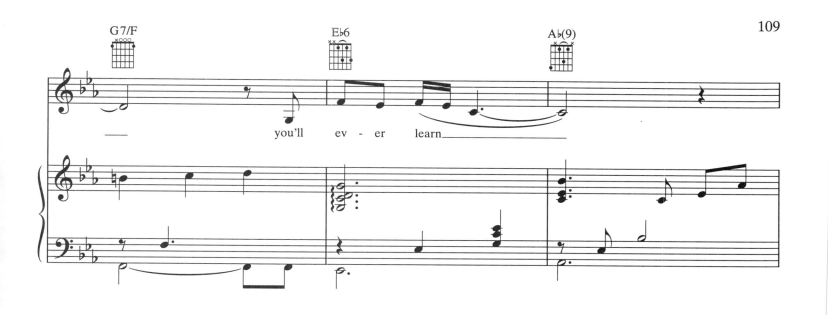

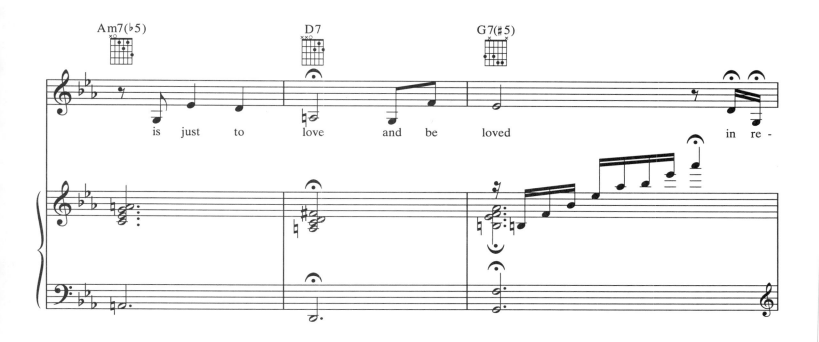

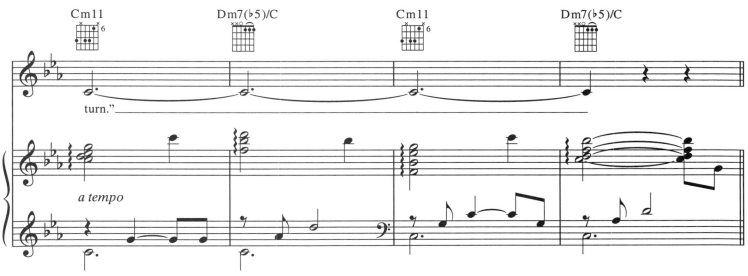

110

Celine Celine Dion

 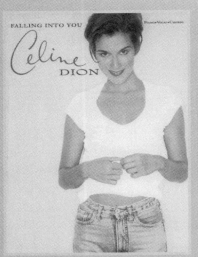  

Printed in USA AD0159 5/02

The Songbook
(PF9520)

Celine's first published folio provides an excellent example of the songs that propelled her to stardom. *Titles are*: Beauty and the Beast • If You Asked Me To • Love Can Move Mountains • Misled • Only One Road • The Power of Love • Think Twice • Unison • Water from the Moon • When I Fall in Love • Where Does My Heart Beat Now.

Falling Into You
(4813A)

The album-matching folio to the 1996 Album of the Year and Best Pop Album Grammy winner. *Titles are*: Because You Loved Me (Theme from *Up Close and Personal*) • All By Myself • Call the Man • Declaration of Love • Dreamin' of You • Falling Into You • I Don't Know • I Love You • If That's What It Takes • It's All Coming Back to Me Now • Make You Happy • Seduces Me.

Let's Talk About Love
(PF9813)

Album-matching folio to Celine's multi-platinum album, *Let's Talk About Love*. Includes eight pages of beautiful full color photographs. *Titles are*: I Hate You Then I Love You (Duet with Luciano Pavarotti) • Immortality • Just a Little Bit of Love • Let's Talk About Love • Love Is on the Way • Miles to Go (Before I Sleep) • My Heart Will Go On (Love Theme from *Titanic*)• The Reason • Tell Him (Duet with Barbra Streisand) • To Love You More • Treat Her Like a Lady • When I Need You • Where Is the Love • Why Oh Why.

All the Way... A Decade of Song
(0437B)

The album-matching folio to her latest release showcases ten years of this pop diva's hits. *Titles are*: The Power of Love • If You Asked Me To • Beauty and the Beast • Because You Loved Me (Theme from *Up Close and Personal*) • It's All Coming Back to Me Now • Love Can Move Mountains • To Love You More • My Heart Will Go On (Love Theme from *Titanic*) • I'm Your Angel (Duet with R. Kelly) • That's the Way It Is • If These Walls Could Talk • The First Time Ever I Saw Your Face • All the Way • Then You Look at Me • I Want You to Need Me • Live.

Also for Easy Piano
Arranged by Dan Coates
(0442B)